San Francisco
Coloring and Activity Book

Fun for Ages 5-12!

CityBooks™

By Carole Marsh

Editor: Jenny Corsey
Graphic Design: Lynette Rowe ● Cover Design: Victoria DeJoy

1

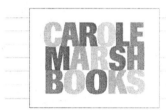

Published by

GALLOPADE™
INTERNATIONAL

800-536-2GET
www.gallopade.com

Gallopade is proud to be a member of these educational organizations and associations:

The National School Supply and Equipment Association
The National Council for the Social Studies
Association for Supervision and Curriculum Development
Museum Store Association
Association of Partners for Public Lands

Other California Books

The Mystery on the California Mission Trail

The Los Angeles Coloring & Activity Book

California

My First Pocket Guide: California

My First Book About California

California Wheel of Fortune Gamebook

California Millionaire Gamebook

California Survivor Gamebook

California Illustrated Timelines

California Jeopardy: Answers & Questions About Our State

California "Jography!": A Fun Run Through Our State

California Bulletin Board Set

California PosterMap

California Stickers

California Coloring Book

The Big California Reproducible Activity Book

California Bingo: Geography Edition

California Bingo: History Edition

California Bingo: Biography Edition

California History Projects

California Geography Projects

California Symbols Projects

California Government Projects

California People Projects

California Current Events Projects

Let's Discover California! (CD-ROM)

3

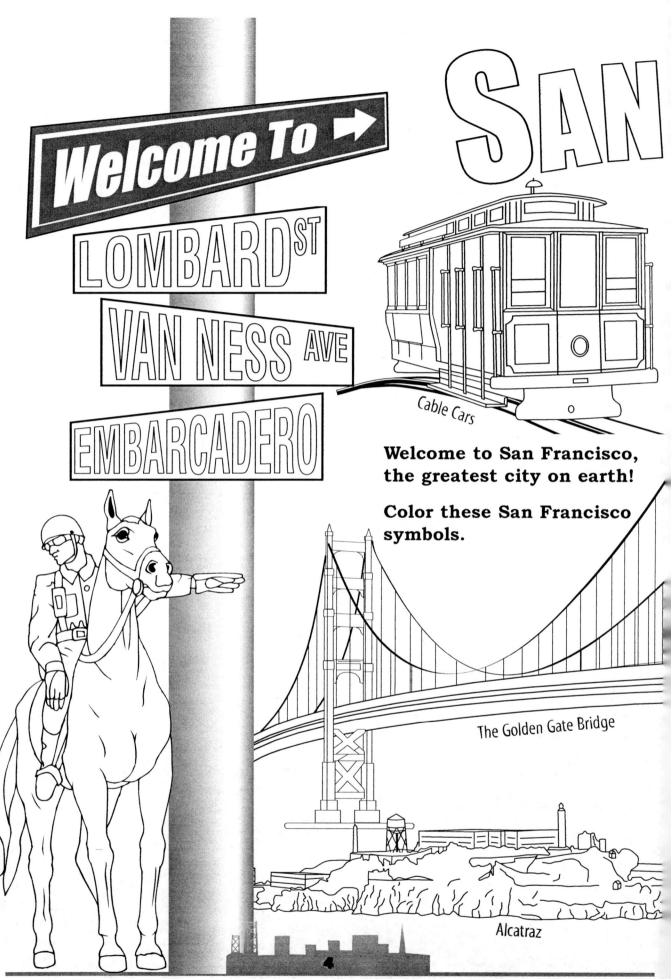

Welcome To ➡

SAN

LOMBARD ST

VAN NESS AVE

EMBARCADERO

Cable Cars

Welcome to San Francisco, the greatest city on earth!

Color these San Francisco symbols.

The Golden Gate Bridge

Alcatraz

4

FRANCISCO

I ♥ San Francisco!

The Transamerica Building

JEREMIAH O'BRIEN

5

Fisherman's Wharf

Rich in maritime history, Fisherman's Wharf was built in 1978 over an abandoned cargo pier with wood salvaged from other wharves. Today it's the most popular tourist attraction in San Francisco. The National Maritime Museum, located on the Hyde Street Pier, includes five historic ships that are open to the public. Fisherman can be seen with their catches by Pier 45. You can ride a Venetian carousel and watch a merry gang of sea lions play at Pier 39. Check out the Museum of the City of San Francisco, Wax Museum, Guinness Book of World Records Museum, and a Ghirardelli chocolate factory!

Color Fisherman's Wharf.

6

"Walk About" Word Search

San Francisco is full of beautiful parks, squares, gardens, and other interesting nature hotspots! People like to take walks, learn about nature, eat picnics, play sports, and just look around in these lush green spaces! Where would you visit first?

Japanese Tea Garden
Lafayette Park
Presidio
San Francisco Park
Russian Hill Park
Dolores Park

Lloyd Lake
Yerba Buena Gardens
Strawberry Hill
Marina Green
Strybing Arboretum
Huntington Park

```
S S T R Y B I N G A R B O R E T U M S P
M C L V M C W I L L S L P I F L L C R L
J A P A N E S E T E A G A R D E N E A A
D L R F L D N K Z O T C V K K D S V T F
O E T I S T R A W B E R R Y H I L L W A
L K D Y N Y Z M Q F T X K L D M X O D Y
O A O X W A F A N F T A O I N W N X C E
R L Q C Q E G I Q D W Q O C L B Z Y L T
E D X A I K V R B S N D Z I E X K T L T
S Y E R B A B U E N A G A R D E N S W E
P O T W L T F T L E X Z T S Y V B O C P
A L F S R U S S I A N H I L L P A R K A
R L S A N F R A N C I S C O P A R K H R
K H U N T I N G T O N P A R K F O M Y K
```

Alcatraz

In 1775, Spanish explorers found a gigantic rock in the middle of San Francisco Bay. They named it La Isla de los Alcatraces (Island of the Pelicans) and used it as a military base and prisoner's camp. After the United States gained ownership of California, U.S. army officers made military prisoners build a concrete jail. Then about 2,000 of America's worst criminals were sent to "the Rock" (Alcatraz), including Chicago mob boss Al Capone.

Prisoners spent most of their time in lonely 5 feet by 9 feet cells. Good behavior was rewarded with a trip to the library, an on-site factory job, or time in the recreation yard. Punishment meant solitary confinement in a tiny cell, without light! Many tried to escape by swimming the treacherous 1.5 miles to shore. It is believed that none ever succeeded. Today, visitors can still tour the island and hear voice recordings of actual inmates!

Liang Wu and his family are visiting San Francisco. While touring Alcatraz, they got lost! Help the Wu family find their way back across the Bay!

START

FINISH

Painted Ladies

Elegant Victorian row homes, known as Painted Ladies, stand proudly all throughout San Francisco. Mostly built during the 19th century by middle-class citizens, about 14,000 of these are still in existence. These homes usually feature detailed architecture, bay windows, rounded trim, and brightly painted exteriors. The six most famous Painted Ladies of Alamo Square, known as "Postcard Row" are often photographed.

Color the "painted lady".

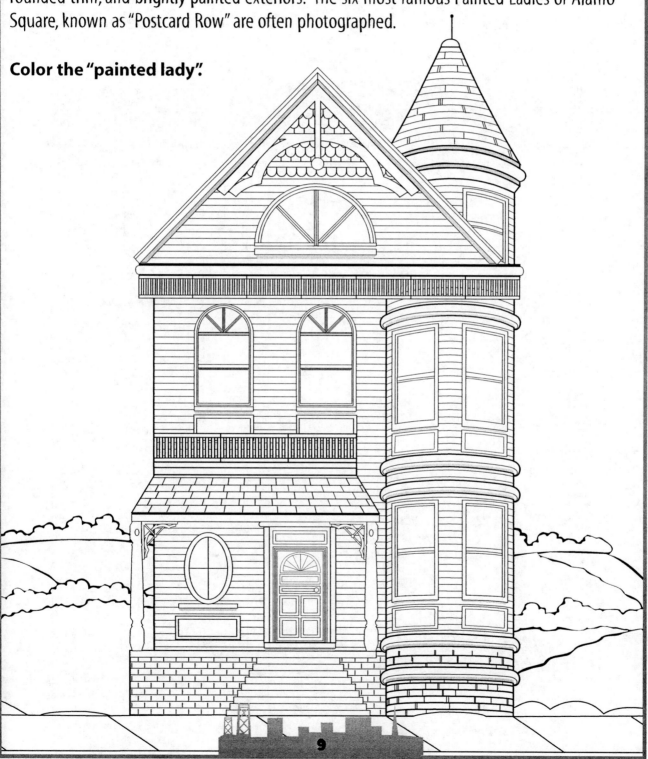

9

San Francisco Museums

Use the Word Bank to solve the crossword. Hint: "San Francisco" is abbreviated to "SF" in the crossword answers.

Word Bank

Treasure Island Museum	Palace of Fine Arts	Exploratorium
Cable Car Barn Museum	San Francisco Jewish Museum	Mexican Museum
San Francisco Museum Of Modern Art	Museo Italo Americano	North Beach Museum
San Francisco Fire Department Museum	Center for the Arts	Asian Art Museum of San Francisco

Golden Gate

The Golden Gate Bridge is perhaps the most recognizable symbol in San Francisco. Construction on the bridge began in 1933, and it opened in 1937. At that time, the Golden Gate Bridge was the largest suspension bridge in the world. There is enough wire used in the cables to hold the bridge up to wrap around the Earth three times! Repainting the Golden Gate Bridge requires 10,000 gallons of paint over the course of each year! Golden Gate Park is one of the largest city parks in the United States. It stretches 52 blocks long and covers 1,040 acres. Ending at the Pacific Ocean shoreline, the park includes lakes, winding bike paths, and several other fantastic places to visit!

Color the Golden Gate Bridge and scenes from Golden Gate Park.

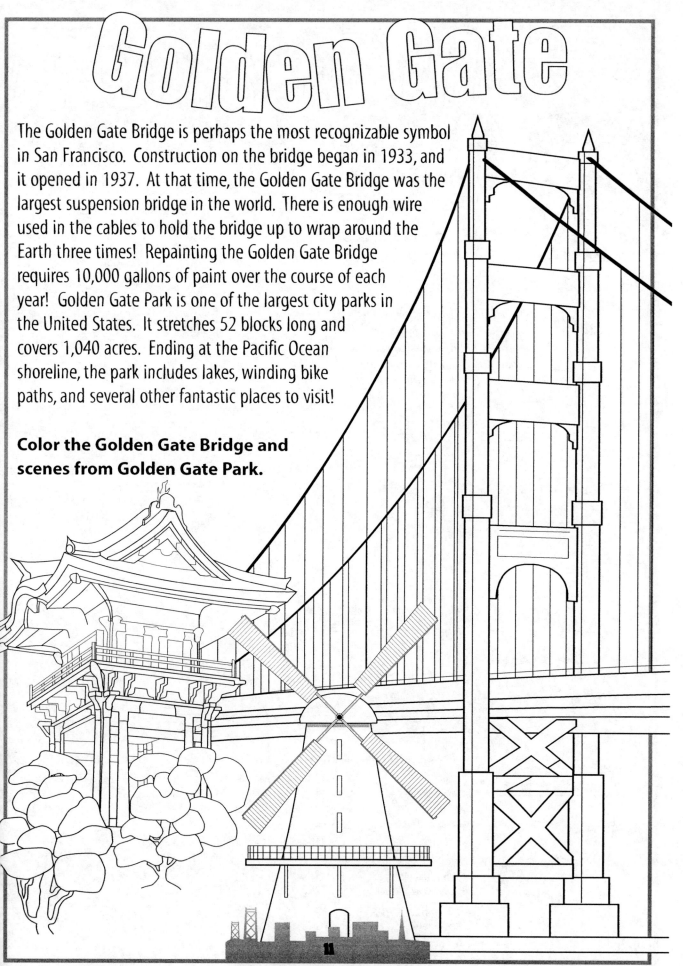

11

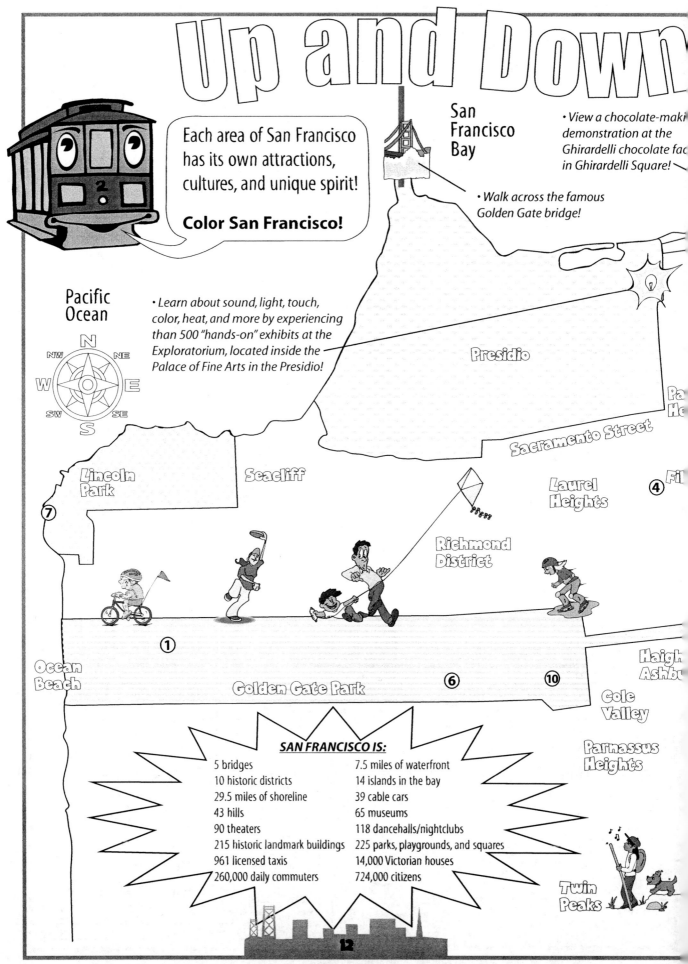

Up and Down

Each area of San Francisco has its own attractions, cultures, and unique spirit!

Color San Francisco!

San Francisco Bay

• View a chocolate-maki[ng] demonstration at the Ghirardelli chocolate fac[tory] in Ghirardelli Square!

• Walk across the famous Golden Gate bridge!

Pacific Ocean

• Learn about sound, light, touch, color, heat, and more by experiencing than 500 "hands-on" exhibits at the Exploratorium, located inside the Palace of Fine Arts in the Presidio!

Presidio

Pa[cific] He[ights]

Sacramento Street

Lincoln Park

Seacliff

Laurel Heights

④ Fi[...]

⑦

Richmond District

Ocean Beach

①

⑥ ⑩

Golden Gate Park

Haigh[t] Ashbu[ry]

Cole Valley

Parnassus Heights

SAN FRANCISCO IS:

5 bridges	7.5 miles of waterfront
10 historic districts	14 islands in the bay
29.5 miles of shoreline	39 cable cars
43 hills	65 museums
90 theaters	118 dancehalls/nightclubs
215 historic landmark buildings	225 parks, playgrounds, and squares
961 licensed taxis	14,000 Victorian houses
260,000 daily commuters	724,000 citizens

Twin Peaks

12

San Francisco!

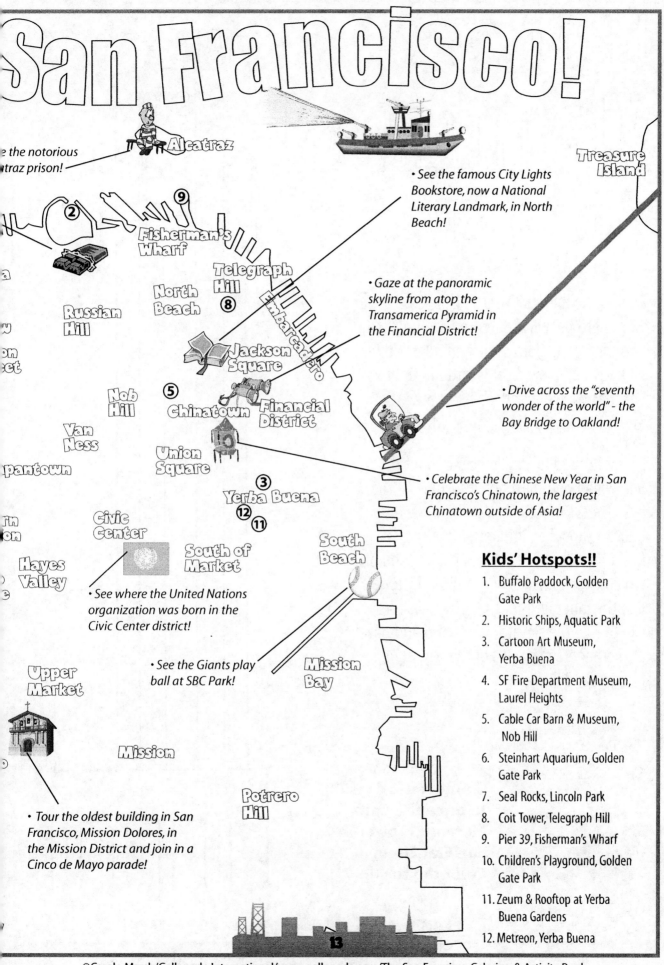

e the notorious
traz prison!

Alcatraz

• See the famous City Lights Bookstore, now a National Literary Landmark, in North Beach!

Treasure Island

② ⑨

Fisherman's Wharf

Telegraph Hill
⑧

North Beach

Russian Hill

• Gaze at the panoramic skyline from atop the Transamerica Pyramid in the Financial District!

Embarcadero

Jackson Square

⑤

Nob Hill

Chinatown

Financial District

• Drive across the "seventh wonder of the world" - the Bay Bridge to Oakland!

Van Ness

pantown

Union Square

③

Yerba Buena
⑫ ⑪

• Celebrate the Chinese New Year in San Francisco's Chinatown, the largest Chinatown outside of Asia!

Civic Center

South of Market

South Beach

Hayes Valley

• See where the United Nations organization was born in the Civic Center district!

Kids' Hotspots!!

1. Buffalo Paddock, Golden Gate Park
2. Historic Ships, Aquatic Park
3. Cartoon Art Museum, Yerba Buena
4. SF Fire Department Museum, Laurel Heights
5. Cable Car Barn & Museum, Nob Hill
6. Steinhart Aquarium, Golden Gate Park
7. Seal Rocks, Lincoln Park
8. Coit Tower, Telegraph Hill
9. Pier 39, Fisherman's Wharf
10. Children's Playground, Golden Gate Park
11. Zeum & Rooftop at Yerba Buena Gardens
12. Metreon, Yerba Buena

Upper Market

• See the Giants play ball at SBC Park!

Mission Bay

Mission

Potrero Hill

• Tour the oldest building in San Francisco, Mission Dolores, in the Mission District and join in a Cinco de Mayo parade!

13

Coit Memorial Tower

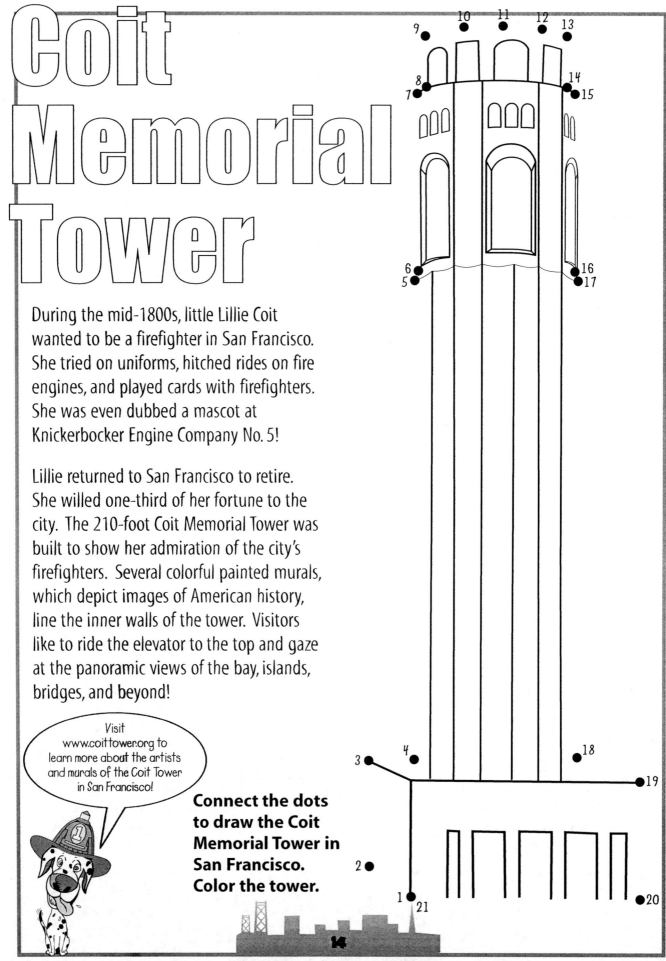

During the mid-1800s, little Lillie Coit wanted to be a firefighter in San Francisco. She tried on uniforms, hitched rides on fire engines, and played cards with firefighters. She was even dubbed a mascot at Knickerbocker Engine Company No. 5!

Lillie returned to San Francisco to retire. She willed one-third of her fortune to the city. The 210-foot Coit Memorial Tower was built to show her admiration of the city's firefighters. Several colorful painted murals, which depict images of American history, line the inner walls of the tower. Visitors like to ride the elevator to the top and gaze at the panoramic views of the bay, islands, bridges, and beyond!

Visit www.coittower.org to learn more about the artists and murals of the Coit Tower in San Francisco!

Connect the dots to draw the Coit Memorial Tower in San Francisco. Color the tower.

14

San Francisco Cultures

San Francisco is one of the most diverse cities in the world, partly because the 1800s California Gold Rush attracted people from every state, nation, and race in America! People of every shape, size, color, gender, sexual orientation, and religion live in San Francisco. Anybody and everybody can live in the many different neighborhoods of tolerant San Francisco! You'll certainly feel welcome here!

Color all of the different San Francisco people.

15

Go San Francisco!

San Francisco athletes and fans rule! The San Francisco Giants and 49ers are two of the best sports teams in America! They play in SBC Park and 3Com Park (formerly Candlestick Park), two big sports stadiums in San Francisco.

Color these San Francisco athletes!

All Around San Francisco

There are so many cool places to visit in San Francisco. From missions to museums to mansions, tourists never run out of sites to see!

Find the words below.

United Nations Plaza	Alcatraz	Alamo Square	Grace Cathedral
Nob Hill	Union Square	Treasure Island	SoMa
Mission Dolores	Children's Center	City Hall	Lombard Street
Washington Square	Presidio	Cable Car Barn	Palace of Fine Arts
Coit Tower	South Beach	Fairmont Hotel	North Beach
Flood Mansion	Telegraph Hill	Russian Hill	Filbert Steps
Pacific Heights	Twin Peaks	Chinatown	

```
U N I T E D N A T I O N S P L A Z A O
P A C I F I C H E I G H T S F O A L I
T G R A C E C A T H E D R A L M W C D
E P S L H T I S T C I P E J O I A A I
L A C O I T T O W E R D A S O S S T S
E L E M L F Y P I O H F S O D S H R E
G A A B D I H Y N M U A U U M I I A R
R C L A R L A D P L N I R T A O N Z P
A E A R E B L G E L P R E H N N G N E
P O M D N E L S A I O M I B S D T O R
H F O S R C W K H N O S E I O O R A
H F S T C T K H S B S N L A O L N T U
I I Q R E S F N I O F T A C N O S H Q
L N U E N T L N W N U H N H P R Q B S
L E A E T E F Y S T A O D L S E U E N
S A R T E P X H N G N T B V G S A A O
B R E Z R S B D J K E E O O Y O R C I
W T R U S S I A N H I L L W L M E H N
L S N C A B L E C A R B A R N S P B U
```

Postcards of...

Check out these pictures of cool places to visit in San Francisco! Draw or photograph your own pictures and make two San Francisco postcards. Send them to friends who might want to visit San Francisco!

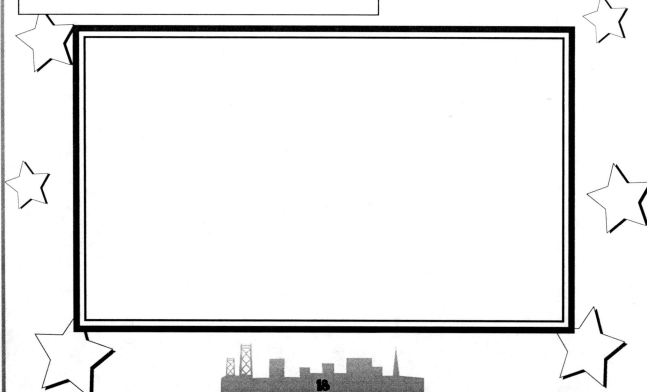

San Francisco

Look at the pictures on these pages. Can you write the correct caption beneath each picture?

Lombard Street	Cable Car
Union Square	Chinatown
Alcatraz	Fisherman's Wharf

Marina Green

San Franciscans love to gather on the grassy Marina Green each Independence Day to watch fireworks and fly kites. The Marina District also features an amazing "Wave Organ" that produces music from undersea pipes and waves!

Color the soaring kites on the Marina Green!

Mission District

The Mission District includes a lively Latino neighborhood and the peaceful Dolores Park. Murals adorn the walls of many buildings in the Mission District, which is named for Mission Dolores, the oldest building in San Francisco.

It is one of several missions that line California's coastline. Spaniards José Moraga and Fray Francisco Palóu founded Mission Dolores in 1776. Settlers dedicated the church to San Francisco de Assisi in 1791. The original bells hang above the vestibule, and four-foot thick adobe walls have protected the   mission from many natural disasters.

Color the mission.

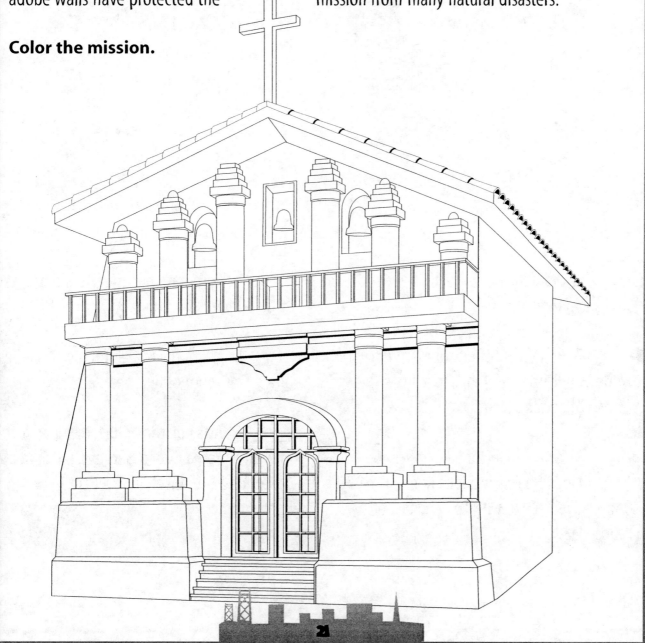

Exploring the

There are tons of exciting things to do in San Francisco! From museums to music, San Francisco never stops moving!

A. Morrison Planetarium

B. California Palace of the Legion of Honor

C. Steinhart Aquarium

D. Lombard Street

E. American Conservatory Theater

F. Grace Cathedral

_____ 1. Dramatic performance venue for actors and directors

_____ 2. Retired 300-foot submarine from World War II, open for tours, that sits at Pier 45 on Fisherman's Wharf

_____ 3. Where many of San Francisco's 12,000 Japanese live; includes Konko Kyo Temple, Japan Center, Peace Pagoda, and Peace Plaza

_____ 4. Corporate headquarters of the Levi Strauss blue jeans company

_____ 5. Memorial to Californian casualties of war; museum of European art

_____ 6. Artsy district which includes several museums: Yerba Buena Gardens, a Children's Center, and the Ansel Adams Center for Photography

22

City by the Bay

Match each San Francisco attraction with the correct description.

G. Japantown

J. San Francisco Zoo

H. Levi's Plaza

K. SoMa (South of Market Street)

I. Candlestick Park

L. USS Pampanito

_____ 7. Famous older stadium in San Francisco that survived an earthquake during the World Series

_____ 8. World's most curvy street, full of hairpin turns along a hilly cobblestone roadway, passes houses built with intricate architecture

_____ 9. Where the wild animals play in San Francisco

_____ 10. Contains dolphins, seals, penguins, a manatee, giant sea bass, blowfish, sharks, 208 tanks of phosphorescent fish, and even "talking fish"

_____ 11. Hosts starry sky shows and Laserium concerts

_____ 12. Architecturally elegant church completed in 1964

23

Chinatown

San Francisco celebrates the Chinese New Year in January or February with a loud parade downtown and into Chinatown, the largest one in the U.S. Thousands of people come out to see the 180-foot dragon carried by three teams of 22 men through the streets. Children enjoy firecrackers during the festivities. Everyone cheers to welcome the New Year as lions dance and spirits soar!

Color the Chinese New Year!

24